AF366642

Crooked Crowns
Shine Too

Jamica Ashley Whitaker

Crooked Crowns Shine Too © 2023

Jamica Ashley Whitaker

All rights reserved.

No part of this publication may be reproduced, stored in a retrieval system, or transmitted, in any form or by any means, electronic, mechanical, photocopying, recording or otherwise, without the prior written permission of the presenters.

Jamica Ashley Whitaker asserts the moral right to be identified as the author of this work.

Presentation by *BookLeaf Publishing*

Web: www.bookleafpub.com

E-mail: info@bookleafpub.com

ISBN: 9789358312911

First edition 2023

This collection is dedicated to

*My son, Kendrick, whose existence makes
me do better everyday,*

*the generations before me whose voices
were silenced and*

*the Black women who learned later that
they have always been good enough.*

ACKNOWLEDGEMENT

Jessica Courtney has been an ongoing source of love and support for me as a woman and as a writer. Kenny has always encouraged my writing and knew that this book was waiting to be written.

To Ms. Jaki Shelton Green, the North Carolina Poet Laureate, who took the time to help me find my voice when no one else would; Dr. Reginald Watson, an English professor at East Carolina University, who taught me how to rethink what I imagined; Mr. Kip Branch, my journalism professor at Elizabeth City State University, who let me be and kept me on the writing path ...

To the publications that gave me space to speak my truth and speak to the lives of others ...

To the experiences that fueled my pencil and burned themselves into my soul ...

I couldn't have done this without and I am forever grateful.

PREFACE

I've spent a large part of my life feeling misunderstood. The perpetual round peg trying to fit into a square hole. Trying to fit where I didn't know I didn't belong. This extended confusion was both internal and external, so whenever an external misunderstanding took place, it fed deeply rooted insecurities and forced me to question my own reality. This collection is a reflection of my growth through the confusion and into the beauty of my existence.

Pass the Crown

Sista, you are royal.
In stature and demeanor, attitude and aptitude.
A queen doesn't need a pedestal to be worthy of
it all.
Pass the crown,
straight and steady or
tilted and secure
make sure it fits before she walks into a room.
Give her flowers that are sweet and fragrant,
with petals as beautiful and delicate as her
so when the world shovels shit her way,
she firmly knows that
she is loved and valued, precious and delicate.

Let her know that you've got her back,
when the headwinds whistle with fierceness
and the ground begins to tremble,
as she recovers from the depths that swallow
men whole and escapades that span decades.
Remind our sista that she is strengthened by the
sacrifices of millions of mothers who only sang
the blues and fueled by the hopes of little Black
girls who wished someone wanted to be like
them.

Sit with her and reminisce.
Of the time that the clouds descended and she
took the hands of ghosts,
walked with spirits and cried their tears;
when she offered them solace that this life could
never give,
when deja vu winked at her and said,
"If others could see the you that I see,
how different things would be.
But the crown I have for you is for you alone.
Wear it proudly and with your head held high."

Crowns
of gold and platinum,
jewels and gems,
roses and thorns,
planets and star systems,
seashells and treasures of the deep,

affirmations and admiration,
appreciation and acknowledgement
cornrows and barretts
lace fronts and fedoras
bonnets and cowrie shells.

Crowns that everyone can't see.
Crowns that everyone won't respect.
Crowns that bear the weight of the world
and crowns that are so light they threaten to
leave with the gentlest of breeze.
With both hands, pass that crown, and let your
sista know that she is royal.

A Walking Meditation

Like tentacles with suction cups
diving deep into the earth
or just beneath the surface
stretched out beneath the canopy searching for a
drop of rain or
a bit of conversation.

The roots.

Some shallow
barely hanging on
as I walk,
traversing the roots.

Stepping slowly to keep from slipping

using them as support up and down the muddy
path.
The path usually traveled slithers beside me,
smooth and deceptive in its safety.

But the roots,
they keep me on my toes,
off the dirt below.
Then I'm reminded of the purpose of roots and
how these roots fulfill their purpose
though trampled upon and nearly forgotten, it's
the roots
that keep the forest alive.
Unnoticed until someone trips
falls and is face-to-face with the roots.

Without the roots, the trees couldn't be.
Sometimes a few look down, back, at their roots
and say thank you.

Rooted

Despite them, we stand.
Tear-stained cheeks, jaws clenched, heartache.
Pray, dancing with faith.

Is This Home?

I am where they prayed I'd be.
They are everywhere.
From the sweltering South
to the rain-drenched Pacific Northwest.
Volcanoes welcome me.
Snow-capped peaks chill my drinks
because They said so.
We traverse the plains.
Run sand through our toes
play in the river
and sing with the trees.
We are everywhere
and nowhere
until we answer the call from the depths of our
souls and existence.
Memory drips on collective amnesia
and we gather everywhere separately
together
in time

to wait on the place we've been promised.
The land that's always been ours,
that calls to us
on ears that cannot translate our mother tongue
and fractured bones that strain to carry us on
cracked skin burned by the sun
and tear-stained rows
of cotton and tobacco
indigo and sugarcane.
We've never been alone.
In bus seats, under heavy artillery,
through malicious milkshakes
and ignorant streetlights.
These places were our homes.
These times
ours
to travel
on a leash
on a chain
in a cage
from a rope.
Our time
to suffer and endure
grow, learn, mature
triumph
then die
in this place
we were never meant to be.

Acceptance

Every seed won't grow,
but they're not a waste you see.
Practice makes perfect.

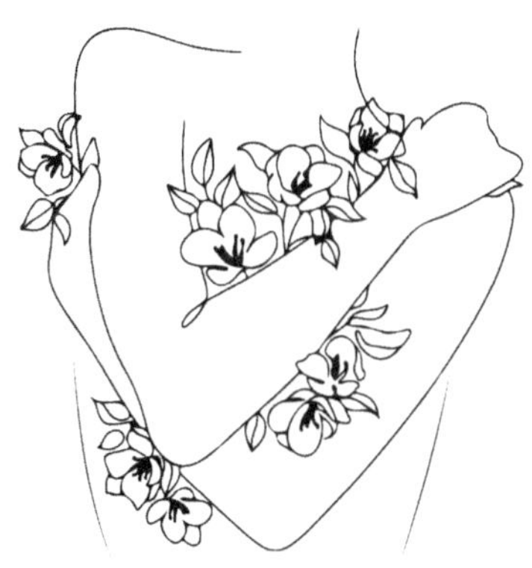

Merit

Unearned accolades
distributed like candy,
prepaid like cell phones.

Hangman

The lanyard that holds
my work ID
feels like a noose
around my neck.

Echo

Sunday afternoon.
The grounds are quiet but churches are full
pews filled with those who think
themselves better than those
they left behind
to cook their food and raise their kids,
clean their homes and tend their fields.
Weathered brown hands pack
bread, fatback, potatoes, apples
memories of babies being born and
families rearranged and shuffled
like a deck of cards
gambling with the lives of generations.
Tired brown hands gather a hammer
knife, a rock, rope
ignoring the raised and discolored skin
that marks a misguided smile

the day the harvest wasn't enough
the day they needed to make a savage example
and those hands and that back were closest.
All of it being left behind
hidden anger, frustration, sadness, and hesitation

Sunday afternoon.
And the last elevator up to an office no one
wanted to be in
down a hall no one travels
dark with disappointment
because I still have to defend my humanity,
my right to be in this space,
in this skin,
but the "exit" sign is illuminated in glowing red
to remind me that my skills,
my ideas,
my silence are wanted,
but not me.
I disrobe.
Leaving my badge on their desk
next to their corporate card
keys to their desk
laptop that weighs too much and
my hopes that this place would be different,
my disappointment that it isn't
hidden anger, frustration, sadness, and
hesitation.

Naked again,
I steal away
to another opportunity for things to be different.

April 7, 2022

Computer keys click away the minutes
Email after email then calendar reminders
A meeting notification before a startling cell
phone buzz.
A sip of water is too brief a reprieve so a social
media break will do.
Scrolling … scrolling … scrolling …

Senate confirms Ketanji Brown Jackson to
Supreme Court in historic vote

An inaudible gasp echoes in office silence.
Time freezes
then rewinds
… at least in my office

Rekia Boyd
George Floyd
Breonna Taylor
Tamir Rice
Atatiana Jefferson
Trayvon Martin
Sandra Bland
Philando Castille
Korryn Gaines
Emmit Till
… then speeds back up to eyes filled with tears
of rejoice.
Silent joy in a white space.
Private happiness in a hostile place.
that won't acknowledge history
or recognize the modern-day witch trial being
witnessed by the world
forcing Judge Ketanji Brown Jackson
to exercise grace that's been stretched across
generations,
under fire that couldn't be extinguished
with a Harvard education,
a career of experience,
or all of the sweet tea in South Carolina or Texas
combined.
While crowns of locs and twists and braids
inch closer to the sky
on heads held higher
with names that sprout from grandma's kitchen

and girls jumping double dutch
a great great grandfather who defied the odds
sisters sitting on the steps chewing sugar cane
and sharing sweet dreams
brothers using old boxes as dancefloors outside
the corner store
a few feet away from the barbershop
swagger slow riding through a neighborhood
with names like Martin Luther King on a road
and Booker T. Washington on a school.
Names that grow like roses through concrete
defiant,
existing against the odds
and beautiful,
with multiple syllables and
beautiful
Black syllables
and beautiful names
that challenge the tongue
with no need for translation.
Names that promise smiles
and demand respect.
Names that travel with eyes and necks that roll,
with mommas that say "make sure they get your
name right"
with voices that loudly demand that you
pronounce
EVE·RY SIN·GLE SYL·LA·BLE
until you get it right.

Names that no one thought would be etched into
the history of America.
Names that some fought to keep from being
etched into the history of America.
Names that will never be forgotten
like
Ketanji Brown Jackson.

I See You Sis

To all the women who inadvertently train their
replacements or stay late or come in early to
make sure the job gets done
Or told that "due to the budget" they can't get the
help or resources they need as everyone frolics
on a company trip drinking rounds of tequila on
you
Or told that "you have so much potential" but
can't seem to grow beyond that no matter how
much training you get, certifications you earn,
after-hours events you attend, mentoring you
undergo, or professional networking you do.
For the women whose anxiety grows Sunday
afternoon and worsens as the sun sets because
the thought of having to wear that suffocating
mask another week while no one at the water

cooler cares that she can't breathe makes her
sick.
For the women who routinely escape to the
isolated refuge of their cars to let the tears or
rage or disappointment run free over a cold
lunch and calls to a lifeline.
To the women who have become hardened by
years of invisibility training during meetings,
crushed for having ideas only to have a devil in
a tailored suit deliver it as his own and win a
promotion
Hardened by having to be a professional damsel
in distress because you know the egos of men
are easily bruised by the experienced,
researched, and common sense that flow from
lipsticked lips
For the women in oppressively combative work
jungles who've been convinced that every other
woman is their competition, withholding
information, or building exclusive alliances to
ruin their careers
To the cautiously optimistic women who
continue to search for sisterhood in a race where
rodents appear to prosper the fastest
For the trepidatious women who form
underground bonds and offer comforting words
and a respite to sisters who are under attack
while staying at the ready

For the women who wander naked in the
shadows after having their confidence, courage,
and voices ruthlessly stripped away
To the women who just want to do their job and
meritoriously climb to the next landmine
To the women who need this …

They don't deserve you. They never have. They
never will.

To the only other woman in the office,
the only other brown woman in the office,
the only woman in the C-Suite,
the other women who are just as frustrated as
you

We welcome you.
We offer the reassurance and validation that
you've been starved of.
We offer you the courage to build your own
table and invite who you want to fill the seats
On a silver platter we bring to you professional
support and guidance as you successfully
traverse the terrain of the boys' club.
With a yellow bow on top, we deliver the
opportunity to coalesce with your war-ravaged
sisters and form solidarity around your
ambitions for more and hope that there is better
readily available.

We offer you the courage and the confidence to
take the first step of the stairway hidden by fog
with your sisters, hand in hand, or arm in arm
We offer you all that we've been denied then
invite you to do more than you ever dreamed.

You can't kill a revolution

They were taken from us.
Stolen.
Murdered.
All we have are memories.
Fiery words set ablaze with undying passion.
A warm smile and big brown eyes.
But the theft of them wasn't enough.
From the ashes the truth rose to the surface on
the breath of hate.
She made it all up.
A white lie.
The change he was igniting
threatened to burn all of their shit to the ground.
So they were taken from us.
Stolen.
Murdered.

This narrative of theft and murder isn't new.

When ancestors were stolen from their cultures
and lands
taken from families by a hunger that can never
be satisfied.
A hunger that ravages nations.
And when those who had been stolen hunger for
their freedom,
demand their freedom
they are murdered.
Stolen from their lives.
Stolen from the comfort they pieced together,
the safe space, the refuge, the reprieve
needed to survive another day.

This hunger feeds greed.
Greed that wants it all because it all exists.
Greed that vomits "you're lazy" when you stop
working for free.
Greed that burps "you're not good enough" then
gulps down your ingenuity and ideas
craves your creativity and wrestles with your
resilience.
Greed that indulges in exploitation
Greed that proclaims "slavery benefited Black
people," to rewrite a history where shame oozes
from its bones and drips from blood-stained
teeth.
Beware the hunger that threatens to consume
itself

when theft and murder are no longer enough
and when those who have been murdered and stolen
rise together and say "no more"
and burn their disgusting table to the ground.

Roadside

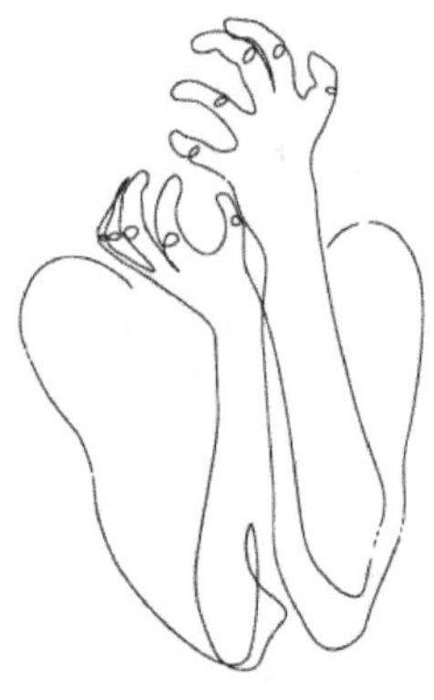

I guess it's fear.
I don't want to give them that much power.
Let's call it caution
that manifests itself through my pounding heart
about to beat a hole in my chest.
shallow breathing makes my head swim and
thoughts foggy.
unsteady hands that begin to shake
uncontrollably
and sweat so much that I drop my license and
registration, my confidence and my peace.

The caution is powerful.
It wells up inside of me and boils, simmers like
granny's greens on the stove.
I pray I get to taste them again,

see my family again,
say I love you again,
unlock my front door again.

The caution makes the sun burn.
Any other time the sun makes my skin glow,
makes me feel blessed to be alive, cozy in a
lonely world.
I wish a sun god would swoop in and carry me
away in a golden chariot because this isn't my
sun.
Caution makes the smells of summer poisonous.
Fresh-cut grass, moist magnolias, hot asphalt,
cool water from a garden hose
poisonous.
I can barely breathe. My lungs burn.
Caution races with my thoughts and speeds
through yellow lights and stop signs.
Seconds drag into minutes. Minutes drag into
hours
it feels
like forever since I last exhaled.
How long can I hold my breath?

Caution hasn't told me yet
if it's safe or if I should flee,
melt into a crack in the concrete or roll off the
edge of the road like a rogue drop of mercury.
Should I stand tall and point my chest to the sky

or curl forward like a crescent moon glowing
against the midnight sky, widowed
seen by many, surrounded, but isolated by
millions of miles?
Tension surges through me as if Shango
commanded it,
lightning dancing from the heavens down to
earth.
Caution makes the tension fiery, unnerving as it
courses through me, unable to settle down or
escape through my fingers or toes.

I'm a battleground, marked by shadows, haunted
by the fate of my kin
who are gone too soon for existing outside the
lines,
questioning when others wanted them dead,
questioning when others demanded compliance.
Caution fills me.
He reappears at my window and returns my
documents.
"You have a good day ma'am."
Air oozes into my lungs. The burning subsides.
Life resumes.

0 to 100 to 0

It's a ride you didn't ask to get on
and one you can never get off.
You sit in the driver's seat
then you blink yourself into the trunk,
then slide into the passenger seat without a seatbelt
and watch yourself surf traffic on the hood of the
speeding car
then slump into deep slumber in the backseat with
your head
propped up on the window, bouncing about with
the bumps in the road.

Signs speed by in a confusing blur

STOP   YIELD
                        s l o w   d o w n

BEWARE   curve ahead

F
 A
  L
   L
    I
     N
      G rocks
Construction zone   detour ahead

The words dance onto the pavement, one letter at a
time
encircling your car and chanting louder and louder
until it's all you can hear
so you turn up the radio to drown out the taunts
and when that doesn't work,
you slowly gather yourself
collect all of you
into the driver's seat … then roll to a stop.
Gradually
until you can name each star and assign new
meaning to the constellations
each name drains you
each assignment takes something out of you

You release your seatbelt and turn off the car.
Exhale as the engine cools,
settle into the seat that you can't get out of
the seat that offers immediate comfort and doesn't
ask for anything.
The easy seat.

The seat that says
just lay here
shower later
you aren't really that hungry
ignore that text
call them back later
who really loves you
it's quiet here alone
what's the point
I can't do this any more
crying is easier
just let go and go

And you sit
gazing down the road
wondering when the car will start again
when you'll want to drive again
how long will you be able to enjoy the ride before
the chaos returns.

Having bipolar disorder is nothing like the
weather.

Redirection

With wings to fly I
would visit another plane
and ask for a map.

Black girl, no magic today

Today, I'm just me.
I ain't magical or spectacular.
I'm easy.
Soft.
Enjoying the peace of a deep breath,
exhaling deeper into being.

I'm not breaking down barriers or building
bridges.
No systems will I dismantle.
No battles will I wage.
Today, whatever day it is, is my day to just be.
The laundry and dishes and podcast will wait.
That email will be read tomorrow and replied to
sometime after.

That thing will be scheduled and those tickets
bought.
The meals will be planned and workout done …
tomorrow.

Because today I fill my cup with filtered water
and an article in Vogue,
a long shower and scalp massage,
music on the back porch and toes warmed by the
summer sun,
an episode of that show I've been meaning to
watch while curled up under the coziest of
blankets wearing the coziest of socks
with the gentle whir of the fan overhead.

Today I
meditate in the moment
revel in the recharge
and be easy
Today I
restore my magic
replenish my glow
polish my shine
refuel my fire.

I feed my legacy and build generational
everything
on a foundation of rest and contemplation,
ideation and focus.

In the stillness is clarity and knowledge of self.
In the stillness is the shadow and darkness
love, light, frustration, despair, elation,
rumination, guilt, melancholy,
that I avoid,
run from, deflect, project, ignore, embrace,
day to day.

Today, in the stillness, I accept all that I am
and envision all that I will become.
And when I emerge
I will be magical and spectacular and so much
more.

The Witching Hour

Drenched in moonlight's glow
we revel in magic's lair
drunk on love, power, peace.

I Am

Only what I answer to.
Kissed by the goddesses
caressed by the gods
heralded by angels and divinely marked
beautiful like fresh roses and a river full of life
and a falcon exploring limitless skies.
Mother. Daughter. Wife. Sister.
SistahGirlFriend.
The one who makes you feel like no other.
Self-defined.
A lady through experience,
remarkable by nature,
unapologetic by choice,
sunshine,
happiness,

honey,
warm and chill,
passionate and calm,
powerfully compassionate, and
unconditional love.

Trust the Universe

The stardust that's me
traveled across space and time
to live again, free.

Répondez s'il vous plaît

May I be your joy
the one who makes you smile deep within your
soul and long for me like no others?
May I be your light
when all seems lost and your path is hidden from
view?
May I be your voice
when you can't find yours or you leave it at
home where it's safe and secure?
May I be your courage when you don't think
you measure up?
I'll show you that you're more than enough.
May I be your defender
protecting you from harm and warning you of
danger?
May I love you for all time
when you don't feel worthy and times get hard,

when things get scary and the clouds don't part?
If you let me, I will.

Love

Sincere gratitude.
Blessings, abundance, peace, health
Creator's got me.

Crown Crush

I've got a crush on my crown.
Nothing comes between us.
No one comes between us,
my crown and me.

Communal tears
when they loved everything about us except us
when families bullied away confidence
when green-eyed friends crossed finish lines
when we didn't know we were in a race,
when they longed for long hair with sass and
curls from any woman but us
and people in the house they said the lord built
told us that we weren't enough,
abominations who should give larger donations.
And we believed them.

Believed that we were unlovable unless the
conditions were right
mistakes worth erasing when we took up too
much space
We were being choked and didn't know we
could make it stop.
Until we did.

We journeyed deep into the ether to
gather the pieces that were us
rearranged them until they fit
fused back together with silver and gold
kintsugi walking
We are our crowns.
We love her.
And she loves us.

www.ingramcontent.com/pod-product-compliance
Lightning Source LLC
La Vergne TN
LVHW041239200726
843507LV00013B/2747